Famous Lives

Showbiz

From Adler to Ziegfeld, from film stars to
ballerinas, this is the story of show business as
seen through the lives of 186 of its greatest
personalities. Here are comics like Fatty
Arbuckle and Laurel and Hardy, giants of the
stage like Sarah Bernhardt and Sir Laurence
Olivier, as well as the more unexpected such as
Harry Houdini, Buffalo Bill and Phineas T.
Barnum. Many of the names which crowd the
pages of this book have thrilled and excited the
whole world, and their lives, their triumphs and
their failures are just as entertaining today.

James Moore is a publisher who has written
a number of books on travel and sailing. He
lives in Essex. Alan Blackwood has been
writing books for children for over ten years.
He lives in London.

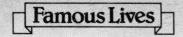

SHOWBIZ

**Devised by James Moore
and written by
Alan Blackwood**

Illustrated by Peter Dennis

Beaver Books

First published in 1980 by
The Hamlyn Publishing Group Limited
London · New York · Sydney · Toronto
Astronaut House, Feltham, Middlesex, England

© Copyright Text James Moore Associates 1980
© Copyright Illustrations
The Hamlyn Publishing Group Limited 1980
ISBN 0 600 33711 1

Printed and bound in Great Britain by
Cox & Wyman Limited, Reading.
Set in Monotype Garamond

Adler, Larry *b. 1914*

American harmonica player. Before Adler the harmonica was
not considered an instrument of much importance. He made
people take the harmonica seriously, as an instrument for the
concert stage on a par with the guitar and woodwind
instruments. He has given performances all over the world,
playing before such important figures as King George VI and
President Roosevelt, and he inspired a number of modern
composers, including Vaughan Williams and Milhaud, to write
pieces especially for him.

Arbuckle, Roscoe *1881–1932*

American comic actor. 'Fatty' Arbuckle was a star of the silent
movies, making frequent appearances with the Keystone Kops
and Charlie Chaplin (q.v.) as a greedy fat man. Scandals in his
private life largely destroyed his popularity in 1921, after which
he occasionally directed, or made other screen appearances
under the humorous name of Will B. Good.

Ashcroft, Dame Peggy *b. 1907*

British stage actress who has won the highest praise for her
performances mainly in Shakespeare and Chekhov. She has
worked closely with Sir John Gielgud (q.v.), but her longest
association has been with the Royal Shakespeare Company. She
has appeared in a small number of films, including Alfred
Hitchcock's (q.v.) 1935 production of *The Thirty-nine Steps*,
Quiet Wedding (1940) and *Sunday Bloody Sunday* (1971). She was
made a Dame of the British Empire in 1956.

Astaire, Fred *b. 1899*

American stage and film actor, dancer and singer, whose real
name is Fred Austerlitz. He started his career with his little
sister Adele in a song and dance routine. Their partnership
continued until Adele married and retired from show business,

after which Fred began his much more famous partnership with Ginger Rogers (q.v.). During the 1930s the two of them made some of the most famous of all film musicals, including *The Gay Divorcee* (1934), *Top Hat* (1935) and *Swing Time* (1936). The slight and sugary plots were simply a prop for immaculate dance routines set to the music of the greatest song writers of the time – Irving Berlin, Cole Porter, Jerome Kern, George Gershwin; and though his voice was basically rather weak, Astaire developed a pleasing and distinctive singing style with such famous numbers as 'Night and Day' and 'I Won't Dance'. His later musical partners included Judy Garland (q.v.) (*Easter Parade* (1948) and Audrey Hepburn (*Funny Face* 1957), while he has also played a few straight acting roles, notably in *On the Beach* (1959).

Fred Astaire dancing with Ginger Rogers (q.v.)

Autry, Gene *b. 1907*

American film actor who made his name as a singing cowboy,
appearing in many films with his horse Champion. After war
service he returned to the screen and also branched out into
television.

Barnum, Phineas Taylor *1810–1891*

American showman. One of his earliest exploits was his billing
of Joyce Heth, an old Negro lady, as George Washington's
nurse – which in 1834 would have made her well over a
hundred years old! In 1841 he opened Barnum's American
Museum in New York City, a remarkable showplace of freaks,
rare and exotic animals and other curios, and soon after he
toured America and Europe with the midget Charles Stratton

Phineas T. Barnum

('Tom Thumb'). He entered concert and theatre management by engaging Jenny Lind – 'The Swedish Nightingale' and one of the highest-paid singers of all time – for an American tour; but crowned his career in 1871 with the opening of his mammoth circus and menagerie, called The Greatest Show on Earth. He subsequently joined forces with James Anthony Bailey, his only real rival in the circus field. Barnum called himself 'Prince of Humbugs', and is supposed to have coined the phrase 'There's a sucker born every minute'; but he thrilled and delighted millions with his inspired showmanship.

Barrault, Jean-Louis *b. 1910*

French actor and stage producer who worked for many years with the *Comédie Française* and then formed his own theatre company. Outside France, however, he is best known for his performances in such famous films as *Les Enfants du Paradis* (1945, about theatre people in nineteenth-century Paris) and the 1950 production of *La Ronde*.

Barrymore

The assumed name of an American family of two brothers and a sister who each had a famous stage or screen career. Lionel (1878–1954) started his career in films in 1911 working with the great director D. W. Griffith (q.v.), rising steadily to stardom with his portrayals of strong-willed men. In 1938 he was confined to a wheelchair, but continued to take major parts in such films as *Duel in the Sun* (1946) and *Key Largo* (1948). Ethel (1879–1959) was a successful actress on stage and screen. John (1882–1942) gave a memorable screen performance in the title role of *Dr Jekyll and Mr Hyde* (1920) and later co-starred with Greta Garbo (q.v.) and brother Lionel in *Grand Hotel* (1932). Their real family name was Blythe.

Baylis, Lilian *1874–1937*

British theatre manager who revolutionised the cultural life of London by presenting serious stage entertainment at popular prices. In 1914 she took over the Old Vic, which soon became famous for its Shakespeare productions; and in 1931 rebuilt and reopened the Sadler's Wells theatre, establishing there her opera and ballet companies. By her great efforts and enterprise she won a vast new audience for the performing arts.

Benny, Jack *1894–1974*

American comedian who worked mainly in radio and then in television. His act was a form of self-mockery, especially related to his alleged meanness and incompetent violin playing, making use of well-timed silences or long, hard stares, called the 'slow burn' style of humour. He also made a few films, notably *To Be or Not To Be* (1942), in which he co-starred with Carole Lombard (q.v.).

Bergman, Ingrid *b. 1915*

Swedish film actress. She made a number of films in her own country and in Germany before being invited to Hollywood in 1939 to play opposite Leslie Howard (q.v.) in *Intermezzo*. She soon became a major star, admired like Greta Garbo for her special kind of Scandinavian beauty and character, and was a great success in such celebrated films of the 1940s as *Casablanca* (1943), *For Whom the Bell Tolls* (1943) and *Gaslight* (1944). With Alfred Hitchcock (q.v.) she made *Spellbound* (1945), *Notorious* (1946) and *Under Capricorn* (1949). A later big box office success was *Indiscreet* (1957).

Berlin, Irving *b. 1888*

Born in Russia as Israel Baline, he became one of America's top song writers and composed the music for some of the best-known and most successful Broadway and Hollywood stage and screen musicals, including *Top Hat, Alexander's Ragtime Band, Holiday Inn* (containing 'I'm Dreaming of a White Christmas'), *Blue Skies, Easter Parade, Annie Get Your Gun* and *Call Me Madame.*

Bernhardt, Sarah *1845–1923*

French actress. For many years she performed with the *Comédie Française*, winning acclaim for her noble interpretations of the French classics, notably of the title role in Racine's *Phèdre*. By then her fame had spread well beyond her own country and she made several triumphant world tours. In 1915 tragedy struck when she had to have her right leg amputated after an accident, but she continued to act almost up to the time of her death. A famous Paris theatre is named after her.

Blondin, Charles *1824–1897*

French acrobat and tightrope walker whose real name was

Blondin crosses the Niagara Falls by tightrope

Jean-François Gravelet. He first appeared in public at the age of five, billed as 'The Little Wonder'. His greatest feat was to cross Niagara Falls on a rope, blindfolded, wheeling a barrow, carrying a man on his back, and walking on stilts!

Bogart, Humphrey *1899–1957*

American film actor, and one of Hollywood's leading tough guys from his 1936 portrayal of the gangster Duke Mantee in *The Petrified Forest* to his classic performance in *The Maltese Falcon* (1941), *Casablanca* (1943) and *The Big Sleep* (1946, in which he played Raymond Chandler's famous private detective Philip Marlowe). Later films revealed him as an actor of great versatility, from the sad but ultimately heroic little drunk in *The African Queen* (1951) to the mentally unbalanced Captain Queeg in *The Caine Mutiny* (1954). With his slightly rasping voice, faint lisp, facial mannerisms and eternal cigarette, Bogart became a cult figure after his death and remains one of the great names of the cinema. He was married to Lauren Bacall, who played opposite him in some of his best films.

Sarah Bernhardt – from a gold medal by René Lalique

Booth, Edwin Thomas *1833–1893*

One of the first great American actors. He played
Shakespeare's Richard III at eighteen. While in London he
played opposite Sir Henry Irving (q.v.), the two men taking
turns as Othello and Iago. Back in New York he founded the
Player's Club. His younger brother John Wilkes Booth
(1838–1865) was also an actor, but achieved fame in quite a
different way, assassinating President Lincoln while he was
watching a theatrical performance in Washington. Booth
escaped from the theatre but was tracked down and shot dead.

Boyer, Charles *1897–1978*

French film actor who went to Hollywood soon after the
introduction of sound and became a great romantic hero with

his 'Continental' charm and soft, seductive accent. At the same time, he aged with intelligence and dignity and continued giving good screen performances almost up to the time of his death. He played opposite Greta Garbo (q.v.) in *Tovarich* (1937).

Brando, Marlon *b. 1924*

American actor who had a successful career on the Broadway stage before entering films. One of his first important films was *A Streetcar Named Desire* (1951), in which he repeated his widely acclaimed stage performance, and made a big impression as a new kind of actor – brooding and introspective. He has projected the same rather heavy, dominating personality in all his films, from *Viva Zapata* (1952), *The Wild One* (1953), *On The Waterfront* (1954) and *Guys*

Humphrey Bogart as private eye Philip Marlowe

and Dolls (1955) through to his portrayal of the ageing Mafia boss in *The Godfather* (1971).

Brown, Joe E. *1892–1973*

American comedian who worked in circuses and vaudeville before making a name in films. His chief feature was his wide mouth which he could spread into an enormous grin. The titles of some of his films happily exploited this – *Wide Open Faces, Shut My Big Mouth*.

Buchanan, Jack *1891–1957*

British stage musical star of the 1920s and 1930s, noted for the easy charm of his song and dance routines and for his debonair good looks which were typical of the period. He also made some films both in Britain and Hollywood, and after the Second World War co-starred with Fred Astaire (q.v.) in *The Band Wagon* (1953).

Buffalo Bill *1846–1917*

American adventurer and showman whose real name was William Frederick Cody. First a rider for the Pony Express postal service in the days before railways spanned the continent, then a supplier of buffalo meat to the gangs who built the railways, he had already done much to create the legend of the old Wild West when he recruited a troupe of cowboys and Indians and produced Buffalo Bill's Wild West Show. After touring America he took his show to Europe, giving a command performance at Windsor Castle on the occasion of Queen Victoria's Golden Jubilee celebrations.

Burbage, Richard *c. 1567–1619*

English actor whose father James Burbage had already built the first playhouse in London in 1576. Richard worked closely

Buffalo Bill with the famous Deadwood Stage, part of his
Wild West Show

with Shakespeare and was the original portrayer of many of the
Bard's greatest roles, including Richard III, Romeo, King
Lear, Macbeth, Hamlet and Othello. In 1599 he rebuilt his
father's playhouse and reopened it as the famous Globe theatre.

Burton, Richard *b. 1925*

British actor, born in Wales as Richard Jenkins. He made his
stage debut in 1943 and was soon recognised as one of Britain's
most promising young actors, especially in Shakespeare. He
divided his time between theatre and cinema for some years
until in 1963 he was starred with Elizabeth Taylor (q.v.) in the
screen epic *Cleopatra*. This led both to their marriage – one of
the most publicised events in show business – and to a number
of other successful screen appearances together, notably in *The
Taming of the Shrew* and *Who's Afraid of Virginia Woolf?* (1966).
Burton's other striking screen appearances have included *Look
Back in Anger* (1959) and *The Spy Who Came In From The Cold*
(1965).

James Cagney

Cagney, James *b. 1904*

Irish-American film actor. Starting in vaudeville as a song and
dance man, he entered films in 1931 and in *Public Enemy*
immediately established his image as a tough, cocky, fast
talking, violent little gangster. He maintained this celebrated
screen personality throughout his career in such films as *G-Men*
(1935), *Angels with Dirty Faces* (1938), *The Roaring Twenties*
(1939), *White Heat* (1949), *Love Me or Leave Me* (1955). He has,
at the same time, been successful in quite different roles, as
Bottom in the famous 1935 Hollywood production of
Shakespeare's *A Midsummer Night's Dream* and as fellow Irish-
American composer George M. Cohan in *Yankee Doodle Dandee*
(1942).

Campbell, Mrs Patrick *1865–1940*

British actress, born Beatrice Stella Tanner. She made her stage debut in 1888 and was at the height of her fame in the early years of this century when she appeared as the original Eliza Doolittle in Bernard Shaw's *Pygmalion*. Later in her career she was invited to Hollywood and appeared in some films.

Cantor, Eddie *1893–1964*

American comedian, nicknamed 'Banjo Eyes' because of his large, wide-open eyes which he could roll around to comic effect. He was a great personality in vaudeville and on the Broadway musical stage long before he made any films, and made another great hit on radio despite the fact that he couldn't be seen. His most famous song was 'Making Whoopee'.

Carmichael, Hoagy *b. 1899*

American pianist and composer of such famous numbers as 'Stardust' and 'Georgia on my Mind', many of them being featured in films. He has also appeared in several important films, including *To Have and Have Not* (1944) and *The Best Years of our Lives* (1946), more or less playing himself as a casual, down-beat but beautifully polished pianist.

Champion, Harry *1866–1942*

British cockney comedian and one of the greatest stars of the late Victorian and Edwardian music hall. Several of his songs, delivered by him with tremendous speed and gusto, have lived on – 'Any Old Iron' and 'Boiled Beef and Carrots'.

Chaplin, Sir Charles *1889–1977*

British film actor, scriptwriter, composer, director, and creator of the world's best-loved screen personality – the Tramp, with baggy trousers, bowler and cane. The child of poor London music hall artists, he joined Fred Karno's (q.v.) pantomime troupe at seventeen which took him to Hollywood and into films. It was with Mack Sennett (q.v.) at the Keystone Studios that he quickly built up the famous image of the Tramp, carrying him through numerous slapstick comedies of the silent-film era and on into such full-length feature films as *The Gold Rush* (1925) and *City Lights* (1931). Starting with *Modern Times* (1936), which was well into the period of the talkies, Charlie Chaplin created a series of new characters, notably with the title roles of *The Great Dictator* (1940, a parody of Adolf Hitler) and *Monsieur Verdoux* (1947, loosely based on the character of the French murderer Henri Landru, the 'Modern Bluebeard'). His last important film, modelled on the life of an old music hall artist, was *Limelight* (1952). He was knighted in 1975.

Chevalier, Albert *1861–1923*

British star of the Victorian and Edwardian music hall. He was originally a straight actor but tried his luck on the halls between theatre engagements and had soon created a very successful cockney image with such songs as 'Knocked 'em in the Old Kent Road' and 'My Old Dutch'. He was known as 'The Coster Laureate'.

Chevalier, Maurice *1888–1972*

French star of stage and film musicals. Like Chaplin (q.v.) in London, Maurice Chevalier had a tough childhood in a poor part of Paris, working his way up through café acts to become Mistinguett's (q.v.) dancing partner at the Folies Bergères before the First World War. He moved to Hollywood in the 1920s and made a series of very popular films with Jeanette MacDonald, portraying everyone's idea of a saucy, happy-go-lucky Frenchman. After the Second World War he made a successful change to older roles in such films as *Gigi* (1958) and

Maurice Chevalier, as he appeared in Gigi

Can-Can (1960); but he lives on most strongly in most people's memories as the Frenchman with straw boater and winsome smile, singing delightfully about 'Mimi', 'Valentine' and 'Louise'.

Cibber, Colley *1671–1757*

English actor and dramatist, and one of the great theatrical figures of the eighteenth century. His plays *Love's Last Shift* and *The Careless Husband* created the fashion for a new kind of sentimental comedy, as distinct from the more satirical or vulgar Restoration comedy, and it was in such productions that he acted best. Cibber was also an important figure in theatre management. As joint proprietor of the Drury Lane theatre, he was the first to run a theatre on modern commercial lines. In 1730 he became Poet Laureate, an appointment which, he freely admitted, was largely due to his friendship with some of the leading Whig politicians of his day!

Coborn, Charles *1852–1945*

Music hall star whose real name was Colin McCallum. Dressed in top hat and tails and sporting a monocle, he made a great name for himself with two of the most famous songs of the period – 'Two Lovely Black Eyes' and 'The Man Who Broke the Bank at Monte Carlo'. He lived to the ripe old age of ninety-three.

Coward, Sir Noël *1899–1973*

British actor, playwright, songwriter and director. He began his career before the First World War as a child actor, but soon after the war started to write the long series of plays and musical shows that kept him in the forefront of show business

Noël Coward

for the rest of his life: *The Vortex* (1924), *Hay Fever* (1925), *On With the Dance* (1925), *This Year of Grace* (1928), *Bitter Sweet* (1929), *Private Lives* (1930), *Cavalcade* (1931), *Blithe Spirit* (1941). Some of his plays were successfully transferred to the screen, including *This Happy Breed* (1944) and, above all, *Brief Encounter* (1945, adapted from his one-act play *Still Life*). He also wrote the script for the famous wartime film *In Which We Serve* (1942). Coward took the leading role in many of his own plays and shows, speaking his lines in a very clipped manner which brought to perfection the English gift for understatement. His many very clever and effective songs – 'Don't Put Your Daughter On The Stage, Mrs Worthington', 'The Stately Homes of England', 'Mad Dogs and Englishmen' – he sang in much the same manner, creating for himself another brilliant career in cabaret, both in Britain and America. He was knighted in 1970.

The Crazy Gang

British comedy team very popular from the 1930s until the early 1960s. The line-up changed from time to time, but the principal members, who also formed individual double-acts, were Charlie Naughton and Jimmy Gold, Jimmy Nervo and Teddy Knox, and Bud Flanagan and Chesney Allen (best remembered today for their duet 'Underneath the Arches').

Crosby, Bing *1901–1977*

American singer and actor, whose real christian names were Henry Lillis. He started singing professionally in the 1920s, joining band leader Paul Whiteman in a vocal group called 'Paul Whiteman's Rhythm Boys'. In 1931 he had his own radio show and by the end of the decade was one of the most successful singers of all time. In the 1930s he also started making films, but it was during the 1940s and 1950s that his screen career reached its peak with such productions as *Holiday Inn* (1942, containing the all-time song favourite 'White

Christmas'), *Going My Way* (1944) and its sequel *The Bells of St Mary's* (1945), and the famous series of comedy-romance *Road* films with Bob Hope (q.v.) and Dorothy Lamour, including *The Road to Singapore* (1940), *The Road to Zanzibar* (1941) and *The Road to Morocco* (1942). One of his last big film hits was *High Society* (1956). Bing Crosby was the greatest of all 'crooners', carrying his gentle, relaxed singing style over into his acting and comedy routines. It was a style and personality that sold over 300 million copies of his records ('White Christmas' alone sold thirty millions).

Davis, Bette *b. 1908*

American film actress whose real name is Ruth Elizabeth Davis. Her long and illustrious screen career has owed much to her strong personality and determination, characteristics which are evident in all her many famous parts. She made her stage debut in 1928, her first film – *Bad Sister* – in 1931, and during the next twenty years gave many memorable performances in

Bette Davis

such films as *The Private Lives of Elizabeth and Essex* (1939), *The Little Foxes* (1941), *Now, Voyager* (1942) and, perhaps most celebrated of all, as the hard-edged Margo Channing in *All About Eve* (1950). In the latter part of her career she has played a number of more macabre roles, notably with Joan Crawford – another very strong-willed Hollywood lady – in *Whatever Happened to Baby Jane?* (1962).

Day, Doris *b. 1924*

American singer and film actress whose real name is Doris Kappelhoff. She was a night club singer before entering films, her first starring role being in *Romance on the High Seas* (1948). Soon she had created her screen image as the cute, blonde, freckle-faced all-American girl, appearing in a long succession of musicals and light comedies, including *Lullaby of Broadway* (1951), *April in Paris* (1952), *Teacher's Pet* (1958), *Pillow Talk* (1959), *Move Over, Darling* (1963). She has taken a few straight acting parts, notably in Hitchcock's (q.v.) thriller *The Man Who Knew Too Much* (1955), though she still had a song to sing.

Dean, James *1931–1955*

American actor who starred in only three films, *East of Eden* (1955), *Rebel Without a Cause* (1955) and *Giant* (1956) before he was killed driving his sports car at over 100mph. But his personality, and the manner of his death, made him into a tremendous cult figure among a new generation of filmgoers.

DeMille, Cecil B. *1881–1959*

American film producer and director whose name is forever linked with some of the greatest screen spectaculars, ranging from his version of *Carmen* (1915) to the lavish Biblical epics *Samson and Delilah* (1949) and *The Ten Commandments* (1956).

James Dean, in a scene from Rebel Without a Cause

De Valois, Dame Ninette *b. 1898*

Irish-born dancer and choreographer – real name Edris Stannus – who was one of the founding figures of British ballet. After several distinguished years as a dancer with the Diaghilev (q.v.) Ballet she formed, in 1931, the Vic-Wells Ballet in London, achieving the highest standards for her new company with such productions as *The Haunted Ballroom* and *Checkmate* (with music by Sir Arthur Bliss). In 1946 her original company moved to Covent Garden, becoming the Royal Ballet in 1956. She was made a Dame in 1951.

Diaghilev, Sergei Pavlovich *1872–1929*

Russian theatrical impresario whose early successes in concert and opera management in Paris led to the creation in 1909 of his Russian Ballet company. Diaghilev's great gift was for recognising genius in others, and from the time of its foundation until a few years before his death, his *Ballet Russe* (so named because it was mostly based on Paris, and later on Monte Carlo) became a focal point for some of the greatest artistic creations of the age. He employed such famous dancers and choreographers as Michel Fokine, Vaslav Nijinsky (q.v.), Anna Pavlova (q.v.), Tamara Karsavina, Leonide Massine, Alicia Markova (q.v.) and Georges Balanchine, who revolutionised the actual techniques of ballet; commissioned brilliant new ballet scores from Igor Stravinsky, Claude Debussy, Maurice Ravel and Manuel de Falla, and costumes and designs from Leon Bakst and Pablo Picasso. Though based in France, the company toured America and had several very successful seasons in London.

Dietrich, Marlene *b. 1902*

German film actress whose real name is Marie Magdalene von Losch. She has become a legend in her own lifetime, due largely to her first important screen role in *The Blue Angel* in which she appeared as café singer Lola-Lola in top hat and silk stockings and sang 'Falling In Love Again'. This was in Germany in 1930, and on the strength of it she was invited to Hollywood to make a series of films including *Shanghai Express* (1932) and *Destry Rides Again* (1939). Hitler ordered her back to Germany at the start of the Second World War and when she refused to go the Nazis banned her films. But after the war she was again as popular in her native country as elsewhere, especially in cabaret, keeping her beautiful figure and deep, husky voice well into her sixties. Her latest film role was in *Just a Gigolo* (1979).

Disney, Walt *1901–1966*

American film maker. He started to produce short cartoon films with a small team of artists in 1923, and in 1928 created the world-famous character Mickey Mouse. Mickey appeared in two silent cartoons and then in sound in *Steamboat Willie*, his high-pitched little voice being supplied by Disney himself.

Walt Disney

Other celebrated characters followed, notably Donald Duck in 1934. At about this time Disney also made a series called *Silly Symphonies* which included the *Three Little Pigs*. In 1937 he produced *Snow White and the Seven Dwarfs*, the first full-length animated cartoon film in sound and colour, following this with *Pinocchio* (1940), *Dumbo* (1941) and *Bambi* (1943). There was also *Fantasia* (1940), which combined the playing of the Philadelphia Orchestra under Leopold Stowkowski with cartoon images. Disney went on to produce many more films, mostly real-life adventures or comedies, and such brilliantly photographed nature documentaries as *The Living Desert* (1953); but his greatest achievements remain in the field of animated cartoons. Disneyland amusement park in California has long been a major tourist attraction.

Donat, Robert *1905–1958*

British actor, much loved both in Britain and America for the manner and quality of his performances in such films as *The Thirty-nine Steps* (1935), *Goodbye Mr Chips* (1939) – his most famous role – and *The Winslow Boy* (1948).

D'Oyly Carte, Richard *1844–1901*

British theatre manager and impresario whose name is forever linked with those of W. S. Gilbert and Sir Arthur Sullivan. He produced their first operetta, *Trial by Jury*, in 1875, and later built the Savoy Theatre, London, where some of the most famous Gilbert and Sullivan operettas were first staged. He also gave his name to the opera company that has since specialised in these works.

Duncan, Isadora *1878–1927*

An American dancer who became famous at the turn of the century for her new approach to dancing and who influenced decisively the development of modern ballet. She took European society by storm by breaking completely with the classical ballet approach and basing her performances on improvisation. Mostly she danced alone, later in her career she had some girl support dancers. Her performances were highly egotistical and set the dance world abuzz with comment. She liked to dance in the Greek style, barefoot, wearing flimsy, see-through costumes, which revealed bare arms and legs. Many men fell for her charms, and her private life was a constant cause for society gossip. She was a pioneer of Women's Lib, campaigning against the petticoat and male domination in marriage.

Isadora Duncan, the great dancer

Durante, Jimmy *b. 1893*

American comedian, affectionately called 'Schnozzle' on account of his big nose, and specialising in a rough, but warm-hearted type of New York-Brooklyn humour. His career has been mainly in vaudeville and cabaret but he has made many film appearances. One song he has made famous is 'I'm the Guy who Found the Lost Chord'.

Durbin, Deanna *b. 1922*

Canadian-born singer and actress who for a few years was one of the biggest names in the cinema, sweetly singing her way through such films as *One Hundred Men and a Girl* (1937, in which she appeared with conductor Leopold Stokowski) and *Mad About Music* (1938). She retired from films in 1949.

A scene from Sergei Eisenstein's film Alexander Nevsky, *showing Nikolai Cherkassov as Alexander Nevsky and the Teutonic Knights massing for battle*

Eisenstein, Sergei *1898–1948*

Soviet Russian film director and one of the great pioneer figures of the cinema. His first film was *Strike* (1925); but later in the same year he made *The Battleship Potemkin*, portraying an event in the abortive Russian Revolution of 1905, and this was the film that really made him famous, both in his own country and abroad. Like many other Soviet artists, Eisenstein was sometimes in political trouble with the authorities, but he went on to direct other outstanding films such as *Alexander Nevsky* (1938), with music by Prokofiev, and *Ivan the Terrible* (1944). His striking images of people and scenes, strongly contrasted for dramatic effect, are the hallmarks of his style.

Evans, Dame Edith *1888–1977*

British actress who began her long and very distinguished career in 1912. In 1918 she went on a remarkable tour of variety theatres with Ellen Terry (q.v.) playing scenes from Shakespeare; and during the 1920s and 1930s won high acclaim for her performances in Shakespeare, Restoration comedy, Chekhov and Shaw. She did not appear in films until she was sixty, with a striking performance in *The Queen of Spades* (1948, an adaptation of the story by Pushkin). But above all else was her portrayal of the implacable Lady Bracknell in the 1952 film version of Oscar Wilde's *The Importance of Being Earnest*. She was made a Dame in 1946.

Douglas Fairbanks Snr in The Three Musketeers

Fairbanks, Douglas *1883–1939*

American actor whose real name was Julius Ullman. He was a successful stage actor before going to Hollywood in the early days of silent films. There he teamed up with Charlie Chaplin (q.v.), D. W. Griffith (q.v.) and Mary Pickford (q.v.) (who became his second wife) to form the company called United Artists, while becoming a star in his own right, noted for his athletic, swashbuckling performances in such films as *The Thief of Bagdad* (1924) and *The Black Pirate* (1926). Douglas Fairbanks Jnr (b. 1908), his son by his first marriage, appeared in such memorable films as *The Prisoner of Zenda* (1937), and continued the swashbuckling tradition with *Sinbad the Sailor* (1947).

Fernandel *1903–1971*

French actor whose real name was Fernand Contandin. He became a professional entertainer in 1922, playing in vaudeville and singing in operetta. His first important screen appearance was in 1932, and from then until his death made more than 150 films. Many of these were never seen outside France, but with the series in which he portrayed the Italian country priest Don Camillo, and such productions as *Le Mouton à Cinq Pattes* (1954, 'The Sheep Has Five Legs'), he became an international star, noted for the comic use he made of his face, long and solemn or transformed into a broad, toothy grin.

Fields, Gracie *b. 1898–1979*

British singer and comedienne whose real name is Grace Stansfield. She became enormously popular during the 1930s for her rendition of such songs as 'The Biggest Aspidistra in the World'. She made several films, notably *Sally in our Alley* (1931) and *Sing As We Go* (1934) which cast her among her childhood surroundings as a Lancashire mill girl and gave her another great song hit. She semi-retired during the 1950s and went to live on the isle of Capri. She was made a Dame in 1978.

Fields, W. C. *1879–1946*

American comic actor whose real name was William Claude Dukinfield. He ran away from home as a child and had a tough time before working his way into show business. He toured widely as a juggler and comedian, in America and Europe, and was already quite a star of vaudeville and variety before making his first important film, *Sally of the Sawdust*, in 1925. One of his greatest performances was as Mr Micawber in *David Copperfield* (1934), and in 1940 he made a classic film appearance with Mae West (q.v.) in *My Little Chickadee*. 'Any man who hates small dogs and children can't be all bad' was one of his real-life sayings, and his contempt for any sign of sentimentality was one of the things that gave him such appeal on the screen. He was also a great eccentric who wrote his own scripts under such pen names as Mahatma Kane Jeeves and Otis Criblecoblis.

Fonteyn, Dame Margot *b. 1919*

British dancer, born Peggy Hookham, who first made her name with the Sadler's Wells Ballet in their 1934 production of *The Nutcracker*. When Alicia Markova (q.v.) started her own company in 1936 Margot Fonteyn became star of Sadler's Wells. She soon achieved an international reputation, largely through her collaboration with the equally inspired British choreographer Frederick Ashton, dancing many of his exciting new roles at the Sadler's Wells Ballet and then with the Royal Ballet. She later gained in stature partnering the brilliant Russian dancer Rudolf Nureyev (q.v.), appearing with him for the first time in 1962, dancing Giselle at Covent Garden. She became President of the Royal Academy of Dancing in 1954 and was made a Dame in 1956.

Forbes-Robertson, Sir Johnston *1853–1937*

British actor and theatre manager. His performance of Hamlet was widely regarded as the finest of his generation. Another of his noted Shakespearean roles was Romeo, being frequently partnered by Mrs Patrick Campbell (q.v.) as Juliet. His daughter Jean (1905–1962) became a great stage actress, noted above all for her portrayal of Peter Pan.

Forde, Florrie *1876–1940*

Australian-born star of the London music halls. She presented some of the most famous songs of the period, including 'Oh! Oh! Antonio' and 'Hold Your Hand Out, Naughty Boy', and two that became great favourites with the troops during the First World War, 'It's a Long Way to Tipperary' and 'Pack up your Troubles in your Old Kit-bag'.

Formby, George Jnr *1904–1961*

British variety entertainer who was a jockey before following his already famous father into show business. He cultivated a

George Formby

bright and breezy North Country style of humour, singing such 'saucy' songs as 'When I'm Cleanin' Windows' to a brisk ukelele accompaniment. He also made a number of films.

Fyffe, Will *1885–1947*

Scottish actor and comedian. He topped the bill in British variety for many years, and became something of a national institution with his song 'I Belong to Glasgow'. He also appeared in some films.

Gabin, Jean *1904–1976*

French actor whose real name was Jean-Alexis Moncorge. He was a success in variety and cabaret – appearing in Paris at the Folies-Bergère and with Mistinguett (q.v.) at the Moulin Rouge – before making his first film in 1930. Seven years later he starred in the title role that really made him famous and established his image as a stern, tough but rather likeable gangster – that of Pepe-le-Moko. In the same year he gave one of his finest performances in the classic French film *La Grande Illusion*. During the Second World War Gabin served in the Free French Navy and was awarded the *Croix de Guerre*. After the war he made more films, such as the highly-praised gangster thriller *Touchez pas au Grisbi* (1954), his strong, manly appeal proving as successful as ever, both in France and abroad.

Gable, Clark *1901–1960*

American film actor who was one of the greatest 'heart-throbs' in the history of the cinema. He had a small part in the 1925 film adaptation of Franz Lehar's operetta *The Merry Widow*, then gradually established his position until during the 1930s he became America's most glamorous leading male actor. He played opposite such great female stars as Jean Harlow (q.v.) and Greta Garbo (q.v.) earning the title 'King of Hollywood'.

Clark Gable

He crowned the decade with his most celebrated role, that of Rhett Butler in *Gone With the Wind* (1939). On the death of his second wife, Carole Lombard (q.v.), in 1942, Gable joined the armed forces, returning to Hollywood in 1945. He made several more good films, but never recaptured the fame and allure he had enjoyed before the war.

Garbo, Greta *b. 1905*

Swedish film actress, whose real name is Greta Gustafsson. She first appeared on the screen in a little advertising film for the Stockholm store where she worked. That led to studies at drama school and to her first proper film, in 1924. The following year she appeared in a German film, then went to Hollywood with her director. Her shy, rather aloof manner was at first a handicap, but it was soon used to advantage, projecting her as a beautiful but tragic and lonely heroine. In *Grand Hotel* (1932) she spoke her most famous words – 'I want

35

to be alone', while two of her finest portrayals were in the title roles of *Queen Christina* (1934) and *Anna Karenina* (1935). The Second World War seriously disrupted her career and in the early 1940s she retired, adding to the air of solitude and mystery that had surrounded her.

Garland, Judy *1922–1969*

American film actress and singer, whose real name was Frances Gumm. She entered show business as a child, joining her sisters in a vaudeville singing act, and was still only thirteen when she was given her first film contract. In 1937 she appeared in *Broadway Melody of 1938*, singing 'You Made Me Love You' to a photograph of Clark Gable (q.v.), and two years later immortalised 'Over the Rainbow' in *The Wizard of Oz*. Through a succession of musicals, including *Meet Me in St Louis* (1944), Judy Garland made a successful transition from

Judy Garland, in a scene from The Wizard of Oz

her screen image of childhood innocence to grown-up star, but the pressures of fame and fortune began to undermine her health. Later film successes included *A Star is Born* (1954), and she was enormously popular, both in America and Europe, in variety and cabaret, singing her song classics. She died, aged 47, worn out by years of strain. Her daughter is Liza Minnelli.

Garrick, David 1717–1779

British actor, manager and playwright, and one of the greatest names in theatre history. He was descended from a Huguenot (French Protestant) family who had earlier settled in England, the family name being de la Garrique, and he married a French dancer. He studied literature with Dr Johnson before making his stage debut as Richard III, and went on to play most of the great Shakespearean roles to the highest acclaim. As manager of London's Drury Lane theatre for many years Garrick brought about many important theatrical changes, introducing new styles of acting, new stage effects like concealed lighting, and clearing the stage area of spectators so that attention was drawn exclusively to the action of the play.

Gielgud, Sir John *b. 1904*

British actor and director, who established the highest reputation as a Shakespearean and Chekhovian actor during the 1920s and 1930s, so helping to win a big new audience for the classics. But he has shown great versatility as a fine comic actor in the plays of Oscar Wilde and Noël Coward (q.v.) and more recently has lent his beautiful speaking voice and sensitive stage presence to the work of modern playwrights like Harold Pinter. Though the stage has remained his first love, John Gielgud has made some notable screen appearances, in *Julius Caesar* (1953), *Richard III* (1955) and *The Charge of the Light Brigade* (1968). One of his outstanding achievements as a director was at the Covent Garden Opera, where he directed a production of Berlioz' mammoth opera *The Trojans* in 1957. He was knighted in 1953.

Sir John Gielgud as Angelo in Measure for Measure

Goldwyn, Samuel *1882–1974*

Polish-American film producer whose real name was Goldfish.
He was one of Hollywood's most famous and colourful figures
from the time he set up a small film unit in 1910 to his
retirement at the end of the 1950s. His company formed part of
the merger that produced the great Metro-Goldwyn-Mayer
studios in 1924, but he continued to act as an independent
producer, being responsible for such notable films as *Wuthering
Heights* (1939), *The Best Years of Our Lives* (1946) and *Guys and
Dolls* (1955). Many comic misuses of the English language were
attributed to him, such as the phrase 'Include me out!'

Grable, Betty *1916–1973*

American film actress. She began to appear in pictures at the
age of thirteen but did not reach stardom until the late 1930s

with such films as *Million Dollar Legs* (1939). Her legs, indeed, were her fortune and made her the Number One 'pin-up' girl during the war years.

Griffith, David Wark *1875–1948*

American film director and pioneer figure in the history of the cinema. As a young man he wanted to be a playwright, and it was the failure of one of his plays that led him into the infant film industry. He turned from writing plots to directing in 1908 and was soon revolutionising the whole technique of film-making with his ideas about the use of the camera and editing. In his hands filming advanced from being a mere novelty to a new art form. D. W. Griffith's two greatest films were *The Birth of a Nation* (1915) and *Intolerance* (1916), epic features far ahead of their time. He continued making films until 1931.

Joey Grimaldi, greatest of all clowns

Grimaldi, Joseph *1779–1837*

British-born comic actor of Italian extraction. He is generally thought of as the father of modern pantomime clowning – singing, dancing and miming with great success, especially at the famous Covent Garden harlequinades that were a popular feature of the London scene of his day. He worked with tremendous energy and dedication until his health gave way, leaving him a sad and crippled man.

Grock *1880–1959*

Famous Swiss clown whose real name was Adrian Wellach. He began his career in the circus ring but transferred his act to the stage, appearing with great success in London, mainly at the Coliseum theatre, from 1911 to 1924. In true clowning tradition he was an inspired mime, specialising in comic turns on various musical instruments (he was really a gifted musician). He also wore a hat which ultimately fell off to reveal his great bald head. Many of his ideas have been copied since.

Gwynn, Nell or Eleanor *1650–1687*

English actress. She started her career in the theatre selling oranges at Drury Lane, first appearing on the stage at the age of fifteen. Though no great actress, she had a light and charming manner in comedies of the Restoration period, and so won over Charles II when he attended one of her performances that she became his mistress.

Hammerstein, Oscar *1895–1960*

American lyric writer and one of the most famous and successful librettists in show business. He had already written the lyrics for such hit musical shows as *Rose Marie* (1924), *The Desert Song* (1926) and *Show Boat* (1927) when, in 1943, he began his collaboration with composer and song writer Richard Rodgers (q.v.). Together they created *Oklahoma!* (1943),

Carousel (1945), *South Pacific* (1949), *The King and I* (1951) and *The Sound of Music* (1959), breaking almost every kind of box office record both on the stage and screen. Just a few of Hammerstein's celebrated songs are: 'Old Man River', 'Oh, What a Beautiful Morning', 'Some Enchanted Evening', 'Hello, Young Lovers', and 'Climb Every Mountain'. His father, also Oscar Hammerstein, was German by birth, and made his fortune by inventing a cigar-rolling machine. He built the Stoll Theatre in London, and several theatres and opera houses in New York.

Tony Hancock

Hancock, Tony *1924–1968*

British comedian who rose to the highest peak of popularity on British radio and television during the 1950s, portraying a gloomy, mistrustful nobody whose efforts to better himself always failed. In his programme 'Hancock's Half Hour' his style of situation comedy depended on excellent scripts, good supporting actors and his own brilliant sense of timing. Later he made films – *The Rebel* (1961), *The Punch and Judy Man* (1963) – but could not successfully broaden his image and died a sad and lonely man.

Handley, Tommy *1894–1948*

British comedian who was one of the country's greatest entertainment figures during the Second World War. In the early 1920s he was in concert parties and variety, but from about 1926 onwards concentrated on radio, his very fast style of spoken humour being ideal for the new medium. His radio show ITMA ('It's That Man Again') started in 1939 and continued, almost without interruption, until his death. ITMA was famous for its host of colourful characters, each with his or her special catch-phrase – Mrs Mop ('Can I do you now, sir?'), Colonel Chinstrap ('I don't mind if I do'), Mona Lot ('It's being so cheerful as keeps me going') – and many more; and it did much to boost morale, especially during the blitz of 1940–41.

Harlow, Jean *1911–1937*

American film actress whose real name was Harlean Carpenter. One of her early films was called *Platinum Blonde* (1931), a title which was soon used to describe the kind of screen image she created – blonde, brash and sexy. As such she became one of the most popular stars of the 1930s, especially playing opposite Clark Gable (q.v.) in *Red Dust* (1932); though in other films she showed herself to be a talented comedienne. She died quite suddenly in 1937 working on *Saratoga* – her fifth film with Gable.

Hart, Lorenz *1895–1943*

American lyric writer who collaborated with Richard Rodgers (q.v.) up to his death, producing some of the cleverest and most literate of musical shows, including *A Connecticut Yankee* (1927, based on a book by Mark Twain), *Babes in Arms* (1937), *The Boys from Syracuse* (1938, based on Shakespeare's play *A Comedy of Errors*) and *Pal Joey* (1940). Some of his very witty and sophisticated lyrics are: 'I Wish I Were In Love Again', 'My Funny Valentine', and 'The Lady is a Tramp'. Mickey Rooney (q.v.) played the part of Hart in a film about the Rodgers and Hart partnership called *Words and Music* (1948).

Hay, Will *1888–1949*

British comedian who was popular in variety during the 1920s portraying himself as a rather sly and seedy schoolmaster. He successfully transferred this character to the screen in such films as *Boys Will Be Boys* (1935) and *Good Morning Boys* (1937). Then in partnership with Moore Marriott and Graham Moffatt he developed his image in a succession of extremely funny films, including *Oh, Mr Porter!* (1937), *Convict 99* (1938) and *Ask a Policeman* (1939). He was also a noted amateur astronomer.

Hayworth, Rita *b. 1918*

American film actress who began her career under her real name, Margarita Cansino, partnering her father in a Spanish dancing act. She made her first film appearance in 1935 and became one of Hollywood's most beautiful and glamorous stars. Because of her dancing skills she made several musicals – *You Were Never Lovelier* (1942) with Fred Astaire (q.v.), *Cover Girl* (1944) with Gene Kelly (q.v.) – but also appeared in such stylish thrillers as *The Lady From Shanghai* (1948), co-starring with Orson Welles (q.v.), her second husband.

Henson, Leslie *1891–1957*

British actor and producer, remembered for his contribution to British musical comedy and farce. He appeared in the musical show *Tonight's the Night* in 1914, and after army service during the First World War returned to the stage to act in or produce a long series of box office hits. During the Second World War he toured the world entertaining the forces, and remained active right up to the time of his death.

Hepburn, Katharine *b. 1909*

American actress who began her career on the stage, made her first film in 1932, and was soon acclaimed as one of Hollywood's most distinguished stars. She has generated her electric screen personality over a wide range of films, from *Bringing Up Baby* (1938) and *The Philadelphia Story* (1940) to *The*

Katharine Hepburn, as she appeared in A Lion In Winter

African Queen (1952) and *The Lion in Winter* (1968); but she probably gave her sharpest performances in her famous screen partnership with Spencer Tracy (q.v.). *Woman of the Year* (1942), *State of the Union* (1948) and *Adam's Rib* (1949) were three of their best films.

Hicks, Sir Seymour *1871–1949*

British actor, manager and playwright. This celebrated man of the theatre was the author of a number of plays and adapted many French plays for the English stage (for which he received the French Legion of Honour). He produced the first example of theatrical revue – consisting mainly of satirical songs and sketches – to be presented in Britain, and during the First World War was also the first man to organise entertainment for the troops in France. He was married to the actress Ellaline Terriss, with whom he made many stage appearances. He was knighted in 1935.

Hitchcock, Alfred *b. 1899*

British film director, universally acclaimed as the master of screen suspense. He directed his first film, *The Lodger*, in 1927, and up to the Second World War had firmly established his reputation with such thrillers as *Blackmail* (1929, also the first British picture with sound), *The Thirty-nine Steps* (1935) and *The Lady Vanishes* (1938). He then went to Hollywood, combining his talents with those of some of the screen's biggest stars – *Spellbound* (1945) and *Notorious* (1946) with Ingrid Bergman, *Rear Window* (1954) with James Stewart, *To Catch a Thief* (1955) and *North by North-West* (1959) with Cary Grant. Other landmarks in his career have been *The Trouble With Harry* (1956), *Psycho* (1960) and *The Birds* (1963). Apart from his very distinctive style, Hitchcock's own special 'trademark' has been to appear very briefly in each of his films, a practice dating from his very first film when he was short of extras and so joined them in front of the cameras.

William Boyd as Hopalong Cassidy

Hopalong Cassidy

Name of a cowboy hero created by writer Clarence E. Mulford and later transferred to the screen in one of the longest running of all film series. Between 1935 and 1948 nearly seventy Hopalong Cassidy westerns were made, featuring actor William Boyd in the title role keeping law and order down on the ranch with the aid of his six-shooters and his faithful steed Topper.

Hope, Bob *b. 1903*

British-born comedian – real name Leslie Townes Hope – who has become the most famous example of the fast-talking, wise-cracking American comic. He was already popular in stage comedies and revues before his first major film appearance in *The Big Broadcast of 1938*, in which he sang 'Thanks for the

Memory' with Shirley Ross – the song that became his signature tune. Other successful films have been the comedy-thriller *The Cat and the Canary* (1939), *The Paleface* (1948) and *My Favourite Spy* (1951); above all there were the *Road* films with Bing Crosby (q.v.) and Dorothy Lamour – *Road to Singapore* (1940), *Road to Zanzibar* (1941), *Road to Morocco* (1942) and several more. Hope has also continued as a top of the bill variety comic on both sides of the Atlantic.

Houdini, Harry *1874–1926*

American escapologist whose real name was Erich Weiss. The son of a Hungarian rabbi, he started in show business as a trapeze artist, but soon specialised in escaping from apparently impossible situations. One of these famous situations was to be shackled in irons and placed in a large box which was then padlocked, roped, weighted and dropped into the water. He was also sometimes encased in a straitjacket and suspended upside down high above the ground.

Howard, Leslie *1893–1943*

British-born actor whose real name was Leslie Howard Stainer. Despite the fact that his parents were Hungarian, he created the perfect image of a genteel and sensitive Englishman, first on the stage and then in such films as *The Scarlet Pimpernel* (1934), *The Petrified Forest* (1936) and *The First of the Few* (1942, playing the part of R. J. Mitchell, designer of the Spitfire). He also played a brilliant Professor Higgins in the film version of Shaw's *Pygmalion* (1938) and had a leading role in *Gone With the Wind* (1939). He was killed when the aircraft bringing him back from a visit to Portugal was shot down.

Huston, John *b. 1906*

American film director, son of the well-known actor Walter Huston. He has directed some of the finest thriller and action

Harry Houdini, the greatest escapologist of all time

films, including *The Maltese Falcon* (1941), *The Asphalt Jungle* (1950), *The Red Badge of Courage* (1951) and *The African Queen* (1952), developing a close understanding with such stars as Humphrey Bogart (q.v.) and Katharine Hepburn (q.v.).

Hutton, Betty *b. 1921*

American film actress whose real name is Elizabeth Thornburg. In *The Fleet's In* (1942) she created the dynamic, high-spirited image which earned her the nickname of 'The Blonde Bombshell'. Her greatest triumph was when she replaced Judy Garland (q.v.) in the title role of the film version of *Annie Get Your Gun* (1950).

Irving, Sir Henry *1838–1905*

British actor-manager and greatest theatrical figure of Victorian England, whose real name was John Henry Brodribb. He had to overcome such disabilities as a stutter and

experienced many disappointments before achieving overnight fame in 1871 in a melodrama called *The Bells*. In 1878 he took over management of the Lyceum Theatre in London, frequently acting with Ellen Terry (q.v.) and bringing new life and magnificence to the British stage. He played many of the great Shakespearean roles and also specialised in portraying historical figures – Charles I, Cardinal Richelieu, Cardinal Wolsey, Becket, Louis XI, Peter the Great, Robespierre. He made several tours of America and was the first actor to be knighted for his services to the theatre, in 1895.

Jolson, Al *1883–1950*

Russian-born American singing star whose real name was either Asa Yoelson or Joseph Rosenblatt. He was a big success in vaudeville and Broadway musical shows during the early years of the century, often appearing with a blacked-up face and large white gloves in the popular 'coloured coon' image of the day. He was also one of the first big recording stars. In 1925 he made two short novelty films singing some of his hit songs, and two years later – after the part had been turned down by George Jessel and Eddie Cantor (q.v.) – starred in the first commercially-released sound feature film, *The Jazz Singer*. Apart from his singing, he made cinema history with his first spoken words, 'You ain't heard nothing yet!' The next year he made *The Singing Fool*, and other films followed. In 1946 he dubbed the songs in *The Jolson Story*, with Larry Parks in the title role. Jolson was a larger-than-life personality who projected himself with tremendous gusto through such famous numbers as 'Swanee', 'April Showers' and 'Sonny Boy'.

Karloff, Boris *1887–1969*

British-born film actor – real name William Henry Pratt – who became Hollywood's most celebrated purveyor of screen horror. He was destined for the British diplomatic service but went to Canada in 1909, gradually making his way into the theatre and then into films. His big break came in 1930 with a

Boris Karloff as Frankenstein's monster

film called *The Criminal Code*, and the next year he was cast in the role that made him famous – as the terrifying but also pitiful man-made monster in *Frankenstein*. Karloff was a master of make-up, which he used to great effect in many other films, but he also sometimes appeared as himself – a tall, grave, dignified man with a fine speaking voice.

Karno, Fred *1866–1941*

British showman whose real name was Wescott. He was in a music hall acrobatic act before forming a pantomime troupe that toured both Britain and the United States. His name remains famous because his troupe included such people as Charlie Chaplin (q.v.) and Stan Laurel (q.v.) who carried his style of slapstick comedy into the cinema with such immense success.

Danny Kaye

Kaye, Danny *b. 1913*

American comedian, whose real name is David Daniel Kaminsky. He had a successful career in cabaret and on the

Broadway stage before he made his first film, *Up In Arms*, in 1944. This brought him instant international fame as a boyish, golden-headed mimic and led quickly to *Wonder Boy* (1945), *The Kid from Brooklyn* (1946) and *The Secret Life of Walter Mitty* (1947). Later films have included *Hans Christian Andersen* (1952). He is now well known for his work on behalf of UNICEF – the United Nations International Children's Emergency Fund.

Kean, Edmund *c. 1788–1833*

British actor who was brought up as an orphan. He was still a child when he first appeared on a stage, and after years of hard theatrical work finally achieved fame in 1814 with his performance at the Drury Lane theatre, London, as Shylock in *The Merchant of Venice*. From then on he was in great demand playing the well-known villains of English drama – Shakespeare's Richard III, Macbeth and Iago, and Barabas in Marlowe's *The Jew of Malta*. However, hard living and extravagance wore him down and he died, still relatively young.

Keaton, Joseph Francis 'Buster' *1895–1966*

American comic film actor and director. Nicknamed 'The Great Stone Face', Buster Keaton was born into show business and joined the family vaudeville acrobatic act as a child. He began making short films with 'Fatty' Arbuckle (q.v.) in 1917, gradually perfecting his style both as director and as comic poker-faced actor up to the time of his three classic comedies of the silent screen – *Sherlock Junior* (1924), *The Navigator* (1924) and *The General* (1926). Soon after his career declined, due to quarrels with his studios and upsets in his private life, but a few later guest appearances and a film about him, *The Buster Keaton Story* (1957), helped to revive his fortunes.

Kelly, Gene *b. 1912*

American dancer, film actor and director. He studied economics but soon after decided to become a dancer and had some stage success before breaking into films in 1942, in *For Me and My Girl*, with Judy Garland. Two years later he made *Cover Girl*, creating a new standard of dancing and choreography that led to the films marking both the peak of the screen musical and his own career – *On The Town* (1949), *An American in Paris* (1951, with its long ballet sequence to Gershwin's music) and *Singin' in the Rain* (1952, containing perhaps the most famous of all dance sequences on film, based on the title song).

Kemble, Frances Anne *1809–1893*

British actress, best known as 'Fanny' Kemble, who was born into a famous theatrical family that included Sarah Siddons (q.v.). Fanny herself was not very interested in the theatre as a child and only agreed to take the role of Juliet in 1829 to try and help her father, Charles Kemble, who was not doing very well as manager of the Covent Garden theatre. In the event she was immediately acclaimed and continued to play there before packed houses for the next three years. From then on Fanny Kemble was one of the great stage figures of the nineteenth century, both in Britain and America. She temporarily retired when she married an American, but when the marriage failed she made a triumphant return to the stage.

Kern, Jerome *1885–1945*

American songwriter who composed the music for some of the greatest stage and film musicals. He was already at the top of show business in 1927 when he produced the score of *Show Boat* which followed its huge stage success by being filmed three times (in 1929, 1936 and 1951); and during the 1930s he wrote the music for some of Fred Astaire's (q.v.) best films. His songs include 'Old Man River', 'Lovely to Look At', 'Smoke Gets in

Jerome Kern

Your Eyes', 'The Way You Look Tonight', 'All the Things You Are', 'The Last Time I Saw Paris' and 'Long Ago and Far Away'. A film was made about him – *Till the Clouds Roll By* – shortly before he died.

King, Hetty *1883–1972*

British music hall artiste and one of the most famous male impersonators who were popular in music hall around the turn of the century. Her own speciality was a sailor's uniform, in which she sang 'All the Nice Girls Love a Sailor'. She continued to make stage appearances almost up to the time of her death, aged eighty-nine.

Korda, Sir Alexander *1893–1956*

Hungarian-born film director and producer whose real name was Sandor Kellner. He made his first film, in Hungary, in 1914, left the country five years later, and after making films in Vienna, Berlin and Hollywood, settled in Britain during the

1930s. To this period of his life belong such famous films as *The Private Life of Henry VIII* (1933) and *Things To Come* (1936, based on the novel by H. G. Wells, with music by Sir Arthur Bliss). Korda then did some work in Hollywood but returned to Britain during the Second World War. He did much to raise the reputation of the British film industry and was the first film-maker to be knighted.

Ladd, Alan *1913–1964*

American film actor who had taken minor parts for several years before making his name playing opposite Veronica Lake as the tight-lipped killer in *This Gun for Hire* (1942). He repeated his partnership with her in *The Glass Key* (1942) and other popular thrillers of the 1940s, then created his greatest role as the lonely cowboy gunman in *Shane* (1953). His tough screen image was achieved despite the fact that he was only 5ft 6in tall and wore shoes with special platforms to increase his height.

Lane, Lupino *1892–1959*

British variety artist whose real name was Henry George Lupino. Born into a great show business family, he was seen on the stage from the age of four and after many years in variety and pantomime made a big hit in the musical show *Me and My Girl* (1937) singing and dancing the famous 'Lambeth Walk'. Another well-known member of the family is Ida Lupino (b. 1918) whose film career, as actress and director, has been mainly in Hollywood.

Lang, Fritz *1890–1976*

Austrian-born film script writer and director who began to take an interest in film-making after he had been wounded in the First World War. He scripted and directed his first film in 1919 and in 1927 made *Metropolis*, perhaps the most important silent film made in Germany. In 1931 he directed *M*, one of the first great films in sound. Soon after this he was in trouble with the Nazis and left Germany, going first to France and then to America and Hollywood where he continued his work for many years as one of the cinema's most original talents.

Langdon, Harry *1884–1944*

American film comedian. After many years in vaudeville he began to appear in Mack Sennett (q.v.) film comedies, gaining notice for his baby-face innocence in situations of mayhem and disaster. He then made three feature films, *Tramp, Tramp, Tramp* (1926), *The Strong Man* (1926) and *His First Flame* (1927) which were among the last and best screen comedies of the silent era. He did not make the change to sound with such success, though he later, very briefly, took Stan Laurel's (q.v.) place opposite Oliver Hardy.

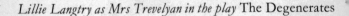

Lillie Langtry as Mrs Trevelyan in the play The Degenerates

Langtry, Lillie *1853–1929*

British actress, daughter of the Dean of Jersey and known as
'Jersey Lily' on account of her beauty. She was one of the first
society women to go on the stage, and though never
considered a great actress had a successful career in Britain and
America. She later added to her fame as Edward VII's mistress.

Lawrence, Gertrude *1898–1952*

British actress who made her debut in pantomime at the age of
twelve and rose to be one of the greatest show business stars of
her generation. She was already well known in musical shows
and cabaret when, in 1930, she appeared with Noël Coward
(q.v.) in the first production of his play *Private Lives*. She took
the lead in several of his other plays, was a notable Eliza
Doolittle in Shaw's *Pygmalion* and starred in such celebrated
Broadway stage musicals as *The King and I* (1951). She was also
active in films, playing opposite Charles Laughton (q.v.) in Sir
Alexander Korda's (q.v.) *Rembrandt* (1936).

Lauder, Sir Harry *1870–1950*

Scottish music hall and variety star, whose real name was Hugh
MacLennan. He was a coalminer before entering show
business, making an early name for himself singing Irish comic
songs. Then in 1900 he came to London and was soon
established in his well-loved role, dressed in a comically
exaggerated Highland costume and giving robust voice to such
famous songs as 'I Love a Lassie', 'Stop Your Ticklin' Jock',
'It's Nice to Get Up in the Morning' and 'Roamin' in the
Gloamin'. He made numerous tours of the English-speaking
world, and was knighted in 1919 for his services to the troops
during the First World War.

Laughton, Charles *1899–1962*

British actor who left the family hotel and catering business in favour of the stage. He was not conventionally good-looking or glamorous, but projected a strong personality that brought him many successes in the theatre. He made his biggest impression, though, on the screen, with such celebrated portrayals as Henry VIII in *The Private Life of Henry VIII* (1933), Captain Bligh in *Mutiny on the Bounty* (1935), Rembrandt in the film of that name (1936), and Quasimodo in *The Hunchback of Notre Dame* (1940). His performance in the title role of *I, Claudius* might have been the greatest of his career, but work on the film, begun in 1936, was abandoned. He was married to actress Elsa Lanchester.

Laurel and Hardy

Celebrated film comedy partnership. Stanley Laurel (1890–1965), whose real name was Arthur Stanley Jefferson, was English and first went to America with Fred Karno's (q.v.) pantomime company. Oliver Hardy (1892–1957) was American and trained as a singer. Both made films separately before teaming up in 1927. They quickly established their screen personalities – Stan, simple, the unwitting cause of disaster and easily reduced to tears; Ollie, fat, fussy and exasperated. And they easily made the change from silent films to talkies; indeed their basic use of dialogue and sound effects added to their success. They made dozens of short, slapstick comedies, while among their longer feature films were *Our Relations* (1936), *Way Out West* (1937), *Blockheads* (1938) and *A Chump at Oxford* (1940).

Leigh, Vivien *1913–1967*

British actress whose real name was Vivian Hartley. She was universally admired for her rather delicate beauty and acclaimed for a number of stage performances, notably as Blanche Dubois in Tennessee Williams' *A Streetcar Named*

Stan Laurel (left) and Oliver Hardy

Desire. But her greatest roles were on the screen. She played what is probably the most famous female role in cinema history – Scarlett O'Hara in *Gone With the Wind* (1939); and later repeated her stage success in the film version of *A Streetcar Named Desire* (1951). She was married to Sir Laurence Olivier (q.v.) from 1937 to 1960.

Leno, Dan *1860–1904*

British music hall and variety star whose real name was George Galvin. He was born into near poverty, made his first stage appearance at the age of four and struggled hard for many years to survive. He was a champion clog dancer, then turned to pantomime to become the classic pantomime Dame in such parts as Widow Twankey. He crowned his career with a Royal Command performance, which earned him the title of 'The

King's Jester'; but he had worn himself out and died soon afterwards.

Léotard, Jules *1830–1870*

French acrobat, wire-walker and trapeze artist who was enormously popular all over Europe. In London he appeared at the big new Alhambra music hall in 1861, performing acrobatic feats over the heads of the audience and inspiring the song 'The Daring Young Man on the Flying Trapeze'. He also gave his name to the special type of one-piece costume now widely used by acrobats and ballet dancers.

Leybourne, George *1842–1884*

British star of the Victorian music hall who was originally billed under his real name of Joe Saunders. One of his well-known songs was 'The Dark Girl Dressed in Blue', but he achieved real fame with his songs about drink, which earned him the title of 'Champagne Charlie', after one of them. He lived a high life for a time, being driven from one music hall to another in a special coach drawn by four white horses – and died young.

Liberace *b. 1919*

American pianist and show business personality whose full name is Wladziu Valentino Liberace. His Italian father was an orchestral musician and he trained as a concert pianist before going into show business. With the piano still the focal point of his act, Liberace soon attracted attention by his gorgeous clothes, the famous candelabra over the keyboard and his general image of gloss and glitter. Piano-shaped jewellery and a piano-shaped swimming pool are examples of the way he has built up an image. Enormously popular in cabaret, variety and on television, he has also appeared in several films, including a well taken part as a funeral casket salesman in *The Loved One*.

Little Tich *1868–1928*

Stage name of Harry Relph, diminutive British music hall comedian. He began as a black-faced singer and comic, but soon abandoned this for a much more original act which included a curious kind of dance performed in enormously long, pointed shoes. Little Tich was a great favourite in Paris as well as London, where there were other artists who specialised in comic dance routines, and was a friend of the artist Toulouse-Lautrec whose drawings and paintings vividly depict Paris cafés and music halls of the period.

Lloyd, Harold *1893–1971*

American film comedian. He entered films in 1914 after some years on the stage, and appeared in a number of Mack Sennett (q.v.) comedies as a character called 'Lonesome Luke', modelled on Charlie Chaplin's (q.v.) Tramp. By 1917, though, he had created his much more familiar screen image, with large horn-rimmed spectacles and straw hat. His special brand of comedy from then on was based on the contrast between his mild-mannered appearance and such hair-raising situations as scaling skyscrapers or finding hamself on the roof of a runaway tram. His best-known film is *Safety Last* (1923). Lloyd was a great stuntman and rarely used stand-ins for his situations. The only accident he had was when a studio bomb went off in his hand, which did leave him with permanent injuries.

Lloyd, Marie *1870–1922*

British comedienne and one of the most famous names in the British music hall. A true London cockney, her real name was Matilda Wood, and she made her first stage appearance billed

Marie Lloyd

as Bella Delmere. She was the darling of the London halls, and also made a big hit in America, Australia and elsewhere, singing such great songs of the period as 'Oh, Mr Porter!', 'I'm one of the Ruins that Cromwell knocked about a bit', and 'My Old Man said Follow the Van'.

Lombard, Carole *1908–1942*

American film actress whose real name was Jane Peters. She was one of the best-loved Hollywood stars of the 1930s, combining great natural beauty with a flair for fast, witty comedy in such films as *Twentieth Century* (1934), *My Man Godfrey* (1936) and *Nothing Sacred* (1938). Married to Clark Gable (q.v.) in 1939, she was killed in an air crash three years later while on a wartime fund raising tour.

Bela Lugosi, playing Count Dracula

Lugosi, Bela *1888–1956*

Hungarian-born actor whose full name was Bela Lugosi Blasko. Soon after he had emigrated to the United States he created a sensation with his stage portrayal of Dracula, based on Bram Stoker's novel about vampires. This led to his even more famous film portrait of the character in 1931, and from then on he became the screen's first man of coffins, cobwebs and candlelight, though he did occasionally appear in different types of role.

Lynn, Dame Vera *b. 1917*

British singer. She began as a child dancer, sang with Joe Loss, Bert Ambrose and other bandleaders of the 1930s, then rose rapidly to fame during the Second World War as 'The Forces' Sweetheart'. Her most celebrated song was 'We'll Meet Again'. She was made a Dame of the British Empire in 1975.

Markova, Dame Alicia *b. 1910*

British ballerina whose real name is Alicia Marks. She made her debut at the age of fourteen with the famous Diaghilev Ballet company and has since appeared as a top ballerina with the Ballet Rambert, the Sadler's Wells Ballet, and at the Metropolitan Opera in New York. With Anton Dolin she also helped to create London's Festival Ballet company. One of her most acclaimed roles has been as Giselle in the ballet of that name (music by Adolphe Adam). She was made a Dame in 1963.

Marceau, Marcel *b. 1923*

French actor and the greatest modern exponent of mime – the art of performing in silence. He has created a special character called Bip, based on the traditional type of French Pierrot, the most important feature of whom is a white face to emphasize the movement of mouth, eyes and eyebrows. He also makes brilliant use of a screen, leaping out from one side or the other as two contrasted characters, such as David and Goliath. Marcel Marceau has given performances all over the world, his expression of human emotions and predicaments, funny and sad, being instantly shared by people everywhere.

Marx Brothers

American comedy team, originally consisting of Chico, real name Leonard (1891–1961); Harpo, real name Adolph (1893–1964); Groucho, real name Julius (1895–1977); Zeppo, real name Herbert (b. 1900); and Gummo, real name Milton (1901–1977). They had already been successful in vaudeville before making their first film in 1929. Gummo never figured much on the screen, and Zeppo soon dropped out. The other three thus became the really famous Marx Brothers: Groucho with his large (painted) moustache and eyebrows, loping walk, eternal cigar and quick, sardonic wisecracks; Harpo, supposedly dumb, crowned with a huge wig of golden curls, and with battered top hat, voluminous coat, communicating with whistles and car horn, also a truly beautiful harpist; and Chico, caricature Italian street vendor, slick, cunning and a

Harpo, Groucho and Chico – the Marx Brothers

piano player with most unconventional fingering. Together they formed an act of inspired clowning, making a series of films which turned all normal standards of logic and convention upside down. The best-remembered today are *Horse Feathers* (1932), *Duck Soup* (1933), *A Night at the Opera* (1935), *A Day at the Races* (1937) and *Room Service* (1938). The large, dignified lady who often appeared with them and was the constant target for Groucho's insults was Margaret Dumont.

Matthews, Jessie *b. 1907*

British actress, singer and dancer who was one of the biggest stars of the musical stage in Britain and America during the 1920s and 1930s. She also made several films, including *The Good Companions* (1933, based on J. B. Priestley's novel) and *Head Over Heels* (1936). After the Second World War she did some more stage work, but became a British institution in quite a different way – playing the title role in the long-running radio soap opera *Mrs Dale's Diary*. More recently she appeared in the television series *Edward and Mrs Simpson*.

Merman, Ethel *b. 1909*

American actress and singer whose real name is Ethel Zimmermann. She was a top Broadway star for many years, taking the lead in such famous musical shows as *Anything Goes* (1934), *Annie Get Your Gun* (1946) and *Call Me Madam* (1950). She has appeared in some films, but her larger-than-life personality and mighty lung-power have always been best suited to the stage.

Miller, Max *1895–1963*

British comedian who was immensely popular in British variety during the 1930s and 1940s. Known as 'The Cheeky Chappie', he delighted audiences with his 'blue' jokes and outrageously loud clothes. He is now regarded as one of the last great performers in the music hall tradition.

Mills, Sir John *b. 1908*

British film actor – real name Lewis Ernest Watts – who began
his career in stage musicals and revue but rose to screen
stardom during the Second World War in a series of very stiff-
upper-lip war films, including *In Which We Serve* (1942) and *We
Dive at Dawn* (1943). He proved a much more versatile and
talented actor in such productions as *Great Expectations* (1946),
Scott of the Antarctic (1948), *The History of Mr Polly* (1949) and
was knighted in 1976. His daughter Hayley Mills became a
popular star.

Mistinguett *1875–1956*

French actress, dancer and singer whose real name was Jeanne
Bourgeois. Before the First World War she was a great music
hall personality, noted for her comic sketches of low-life Paris
women. Later she turned more to singing and dancing,
becoming the most glamorous figure in such famous Paris
night spots as the Moulin Rouge, the Folies-Bergère and
Casino de Paris. Her magnificent hats and dresses were always
a striking part of her act.

Mix, Tom *1880–1940*

American film actor who was one of the biggest stars of the
silent-film era as a cowboy hero. Before that he had toured
America with a Wild West show and left the cinema again to
form his own circus, though he did make one well-known
feature film in sound – an early version of the classic Western
Destry Rides Again in 1932.

Monroe, Marilyn *1926–1962*

American film actress whose real name was Norma Jean Baker.
From being a photographer's model, she appeared in a number
of films while Hollywood built her up as a great new blonde
sex symbol. *Niagara* (1952) was the film which presented her

Marilyn Monroe

fully in this light, but she worked hard at her acting and gave
attractive performances in *Gentlemen Prefer Blondes* (1953), *The
Seven Year Itch* (1955) and *Some Like It Hot* (1959). At the same
time, her career did not run smoothly, and soon after her
divorce from playwright husband Arthur Miller she committed
suicide. She had become a much-loved figure, and her
unhappiness and early death were blamed on Hollywood and
the pressures on her as a star.

Nero AD *37–68*

Roman emperor. Though a tyrant and murderer, he was
devoted to the theatre and frequently took part in
performances, as actor, singer and dancer. As was the custom,
he performed wearing a mask, this being specially modelled on

his own features or on those of one of his mistresses. One thing he did not do was to fiddle while Rome burned. Violins were not invented for another 1500 years!

Nijinsky, Vaslav *1890–1950*

Russian ballet dancer who made his debut in 1908 and was a sensational success during the years 1909 to 1913 when he was principal male dancer in the Diaghilev (q.v.) Ballet. Among the productions in which he appeared were *L' Après-midi d'un faune* (music by Debussy), *Petrushka* and *The Rite of Spring* (music by Stravinsky). In these and other works Nijinsky restored the importance of the male dancer to the stage and helped to revolutionise the whole art of ballet. Those who saw him also spoke of his phenomenal leaps into the air, during which he seemed to hang suspended in space. Alas, the end of his career came soon after his break with Diaghilev. He eventually lapsed

Vaslav Nijinsky

into insanity from which he never recovered. His dancing career spanned a short ten years!

Niven, David *b. 1910*

British film actor. He was a soldier and then a lumberjack before beginning his screen career in Hollywood in the 1930s. During the Second World War he returned to the army as a Commando officer but also appeared in two major British films – *The First of the Few* (1942), about the man who designed the Spitfire, and *The Way Ahead* (1944). These highly idealistic war films made Niven into a big star, and he has made other war films since, notably *The Guns of Navarone* (1961). But his usual screen image of an unflappable British public school type has not restricted him, and he has played with equal success in a wide variety of films showing special charm and a gift for light comedy in such productions as *Around the World in Eighty Days* (1956) and *The Pink Panther* (1964). He also proved to be a witty and observant writer with his best-selling books of autobiography *The Moon's a Balloon* and *Bring on the Empty Horses*.

Novello, Ivor *1893–1951*

British actor, playwright and composer whose full name was Ivor Novello Davies. During the First World War he wrote the song 'Keep the Home Fires Burning', and from then until his death was at the centre of British show business and entertainment. He wrote a number of straight plays, including *Symphony in Two Flats* (1929) and the comedy *We Proudly Present* (1947), in which he appeared as a stylish actor. Above all he is remembered for his series of hugely successful musical romances at London's Drury Lane theatre – *Glamorous Nights* (1935), *The Dancing Years* (1939), *Perchance to Dream* (1945), *King's Rhapsody* (1949) – in which he also took the male lead.

Nureyev, Rudolf *b. 1938*

Soviet Russian dancer who was performing in France with the
Kirov Ballet in 1961 when he secured political asylum and has
since remained in the West. Acclaimed as the greatest male
dancer of the 1960s and 1970s, he has been permanent guest
artist of the Royal Ballet since 1962, and he formed a
magnificent dancing partnership with Britain's Margot
Fonteyn (q.v.) which lasted for several years. He has made a
number of television appearances, and a full-length film about
his life and work, *I Am a Dancer* (1972).

Oakley, Annie *1860–1926*

American sharp-shooter whose full name was Phoebe Anne
Oakley Mozee. She and her husband Frank Butler had already
become quite famous in vaudeville with their sharp-shooting

Annie Oakley

act when they joined Buffalo Bill's (q.v.) Wild West Show in 1885. Annie Oakley – or 'Little Missy' as she was also known – was a sensation. At thirty paces she could shoot the lighted end off a cigarette in her husband's mouth, and during one of the Show's European tours she once performed this feat with the German Crown Prince Wilhelm (later Kaiser Wilhelm II). She was badly injured in a train crash in 1901, but recovered and continued her act for several more years. The hit stage and screen musical *Annie Get Your Gun* was based on her life.

Olivier, Sir Laurence Kerr *b. 1907*

British actor-manager and director and one of the biggest names in British theatre. He first came to prominence in 1937 when he joined the Old Vic company, and from then on has been at the very top of his profession. Together with his strong, assertive voice and athletic body, he has proved an actor of remarkable versatility, appearing in roles ranging from Shakespeare's *Hamlet* and *Othello*, and Chekhov's *Uncle Vanya*, to the broken comic Archie Rice in John Osborne's *The Entertainer*. His equally distinguished career in films has included leading roles in *Wuthering Heights* (1939) and *Rebecca* (1940), while he reached his widest audience in his three great Shakespearean screen portrayals: *Henry V* (1944), *Hamlet* (1948) and *Richard III* (1955). He has also been director of the Chichester Festival Theatre and presided over the building of London's National Theatre. He was knighted in 1947 and created a life peer in 1971.

Pavlova, Anna *1881–1931*

Russian ballerina. In 1909, when she was already a prima ballerina in her own country, she danced with the Diaghilev (q.v.) Ballet in Paris. Soon after she formed her own company and travelled all over the world, bringing ballet to people who otherwise would probably never have seen it. Her most famous dance was to the music of Saint-Saëns' 'The Swan' from his *Carnival of the Animals*.

Anna Pavlova

Piaf, Edith Giovanna *1915–1963*

French singer whose real name was Giovanna Edith Gassion.
She had a tough childhood, singing for her living on the
streets of Paris, then rose to become one of the biggest stars of
French cabaret and music hall. She was a fragile little woman –
her stage name 'Piaf' being French slang for 'sparrow' – but
with a dynamic voice and personality. 'La vie en rose', which
she wrote herself, and 'Milord' were two of her hit songs.

Pickford, Mary *1893–1979*

Canadian-born actress whose real name was Gladys Mary
Smith. She first appeared on a stage at the age of five and was
all set for a long theatrical career when a period out of work
turned her attention to films. Within a few years she was one of

the most popular heroines of the silent screen, usually portraying little girls in rather sorrowful melodramas. Among her many silent films were *Pollyana* (1920) and *Little Lord Fauntleroy* (1921, in which she played both the boy hero and his mother). But she was one of those stars of the silent films who did not adapt very happily to talkies, and apart from some stage and radio work, entered a long period of retirement.

Porter, Cole *1891–1964*

American songwriter, and one of the greatest success stories in show business. He was both wealthy and immensely talented and at the centre of society life for years. A serious riding accident in 1937 which crippled him was the one tragedy of his life. He almost always wrote both words and music to his songs, and most of his stage musicals were later turned into films, including *The Gay Divorcee* (1934), *Anything Goes* (1936) and *Kiss Me Kate* (1953, based on Shakespeare's *The Taming of*

Cole Porter

the Shrew). In addition he wrote the scores for the film musicals *The Pirate* (1948) and *High Society* (1956). Among his hit songs are 'You're the Top', 'Begin the Beguine', and 'Night and Day'. A film about his life, called *Night and Day*, was made in 1946.

Raft, George *b. 1903*

American film actor famed for his portrayals of smart, well-groomed gangsters. He first made his name in *Scarface* (1932), adding to his reputation in *Midnight Club* (1933), *The Glass Key* (1935) and many other films. In *Some Like It Hot* (1959) he gave a good parody of his screen image as Spats Colombo, delegate to a gangster's convention.

Redgrave, Sir Michael Scudamore *b. 1908*

British actor. Though born into a theatrical family, Sir Michael was a schoolmaster before he himself began his stage career. This was interrupted by the Second World War, during which he served in the navy, but soon after he started to gain recognition, in Britain and America, for his sensitive playing of the great Shakespearean roles, including Hamlet, Prospero and King Lear. A later triumph was his portrayal of Chekhov's Uncle Vanya at the Chichester Festival in 1962. He made his film debut in Alfred Hitchcock's *The Lady Vanishes* (1938), and was impressive in many other films, including *The Way to the Stars* (1945), as the mad ventriloquist in *Dead of Night* (1945), and as Jack Worthing in the 1952 production of Oscar Wilde's *The Importance of Being Earnest*. He was knighted in 1959. His daughter Vanessa (b. 1937) is a well-established actress in her own right.

Richardson, Sir Ralph David *b. 1902*

British actor, noted for a special kind of quiet nervous tension in many of his performances, though he has been highly praised for his portrayal of such rumbustious characters as Shakespeare's Sir John Falstaff. He made his first stage appearance in 1921, gradually gaining recognition as a fine classic actor up to the Second World War. During the war he served in the Fleet Air Arm, returning to the stage with even greater success, both at London's Old Vic and at the Royal Shakespeare Theatre, Stratford. Apart from Falstaff, his other great roles have included Ben Jonson's Volpone and Ibsen's Peer Gynt; and he has made other notable appearances in contemporary drama, for example, playing opposite Sir John Gielgud (q.v.) in Harold Pinter's *No Man's Land*. He has also been impressive on the screen, in such major British films as *The Fallen Idol* (1948), *An Outcast of the Islands* (1951), and as Buckingham in Sir Laurence Olivier's (q.v.) *Richard III* (1955). He was knighted in 1947.

Roach, Hal *b. 1892*

American pioneer film producer. Turning from gold prospecting in Alaska to film-making in California, he soon formed his own company with Harold Lloyd (q.v.) and discovered such big names of the screen as Laurel and Hardy (q.v.) and Mickey Rooney (q.v.). Much of his work belongs to the days of silent film, but he produced some memorable talkies, notably *Of Mice and Men* (1939). In 1948 he also set up the Hal Roach Television Corporation.

Robeson, Paul *1898–1976*

Black American singer and actor who qualified as a lawyer before entering show business. His rich bass voice led to important screen singing roles in *Sanders of the River* (1935) and *Show Boat* (1936), though he was able to develop his acting and express his strong political feelings in *The Proud Valley* (1940), about a Welsh mining disaster. In 1958 he played Othello with the Royal Shakespeare Company.

Robey, Sir George *1869–1954*

British comic actor who started in music hall in 1891 and was
soon famous for his stage appearance, dressed in a clergyman's
hat and coat, with a cheeky looking face heightened by very
large and expressive eyebrows. Called 'The Prime Minister of
Mirth', he was equally successful in variety, pantomime and
revue. He also had a career in films, appearing as Sancho Panza
opposite the famous Russian bass Chaliapin in a musical
version of *Don Quixote* (1934) and as Ali Baba in the screen
version of *Chu Chin Chow* (also 1934). He was knighted in 1953.

Robinson, Edward G. *1893–1972*

American film actor born in Rumania, whose real name was
Emanuel Goldenberg. After some years in vaudeville and on

Edward G. Robinson, as he appeared in Little Caesar

the stage he made his first screen appearance in 1923. In 1930 he was given a star role as the gangster Rico Bandello in *Little Caesar*, a part modelled on Al Capone, and his hard-voiced, hard-mouthed performance led to many other tough-guy film portraits during the 1930s and 1940s. But he was a versatile actor, equally convincing as a good, kindly man, and with a flair for comedy.

Robson, Dame Flora *b. 1902*

British actress, renowned for the deep, quiet intensity of her performances, though she has acted well in comedy. On the stage she has won much praise for her roles in Shakespeare, Chekhov and Ibsen. On the screen she was memorable as an ageing Queen Elizabeth I in *Fire Over England* (1937), and has usually been cast as a serious or mature woman in her other films. She was made a Dame in 1960.

Rodgers, Richard *b. 1902*

American song writer who collaborated first with Lorenz Hart (q.v.) to produce such witty and satirical musical stage shows as *On Your Toes* (1936, including the ballet sequence 'Slaughter on Tenth Avenue') and *Pal Joey* (1940). When Hart died in 1943 he started working with lyricist Oscar Hammerstein (q.v.), creating with him some even more famous and successful stage musicals – *Oklahoma!* (1943), *Carousel* (1945), *South Pacific* (1949), *The King and I* (1951) and *The Sound of Music* (1959). All these shows were adapted for the screen. In addition Richard Rodgers has written the music for such television series as *Victory at Sea* and *Winston Churchill – The Valiant Years*.

Rogers, Ginger *b. 1911*

American film actress whose real name is Virginia McMath.

Richard Rodgers (left) and Oscar Hammerstein II

She appeared in two big film musicals – *42nd Street* (1933) and *Gold-diggers of 1933* – before beginning her famous screen dancing partnership with Fred Astaire (q.v.), perfectly matching his grace and style in *Flying Down to Rio* (1933), *Top Hat* (1935), *Roberta* (1935), *Swing Time* (1936) and *Follow the Fleet* (1936). She has also been a good straight actor and polished comedienne.

Rogers, Roy *b. 1912*

American film actor whose real name is Leonard Slye. He first took the stage name of Dick Weston when he formed a group of singing cowboys, then became the much more familiar Roy Rogers, star of many cowboy films with his faithful horse Trigger.

Rooney, Mickey *b. 1922*

American actor whose real name is Joe Yule. He was born into show business and appeared in vaudeville as a child. He progressed to boyhood with his portrayal of Puck in the film of *A Midsummer Night's Dream* (1935), and a boy he remained as far as films were concerned for years to come, playing the part of a small-town lad called Andy Hardy in a very popular series. At the same time he partnered Judy Garland in two good musicals, *Babes in Arms* (1939) and *Strike Up The Band* (1940), and finally broke into adult roles playing such parts as lyric writer Lorenz Hart (q.v.) in *Words and Music* (1948).

Sennett, Mack *1884–1960*

American film producer and director who was born in Canada as Michael Sinnott. From a job in a steel works he went on the stage and from there moved to the infant film industry in 1909. Though he continued working in films right up to his death, his name is forever associated with slapstick comedy of the silent screen. He produced or directed many such films, featuring Fatty Arbuckle (q.v.), Buster Keaton (q.v.) and the famous troupe of clowns, the Keystone Kops (named after the film company that he helped to run for some years).

Schickaneder, Emanuel *1751–1812*

Austrian actor, singer, playwright and producer who was a leading figure in the Viennese theatre and opera of his time. As an actor he ranged from Hamlet to the special kind of Viennese comic acting called *Singspiel* (play with songs); and it was in this connection that he collaborated with Mozart over the creation of the opera *The Magic Flute* (1791), writing the part of Papageno the bird catcher for himself. He later built the famous Theater an der Wien where Beethoven's opera *Fidelio* was first staged, but died in poverty.

Shearer, Moira *b. 1926*

British dancer – real name Moira King – who gained recognition as one of her generation's finest dancers as leading ballerina with the Sadler's Wells Ballet. She reached her biggest audience in two very successful films centred round her dancing – *The Red Shoes* (1948) and *The Tales of Hoffman* (1951).

Sheridan, Mark *1866–1917*

British cockney comedian, a well-known figure on the music hall stage dressed in a curious combination of top hat, frock coat and bell-bottomed trousers, and famous for such songs as 'I Do Like to be Beside the Seaside', 'Who Were You With Last Night?' and 'Here We Are Again'. Despite the jollity of his singing he suffered from depression and took his own life.

Shields, Ella *1880–1952*

American-born star of the British music hall and one of the most celebrated figures in the tradition of male impersonators. Dressed in shabby top hat and tails, and wearing a monocle, she sang 'Burlington Bertie from Bow', a funny and satirical dig at the aristocracy and the class system. Another of her songs was 'Show Me the Way to go Home'.

Siddons, Sarah *1755–1831*

British actress, the daughter of Roger Kemble – founding figure of a great theatrical family – who used her husband's name in her own stage career. She was a commanding woman in appearance and personality, specialising in tragic roles, especially that of Lady Macbeth. She won the admiration of many of the great men of letters of her age, including Dr Johnson, William Hazlitt and Horace Walpole. She was also the subject of several paintings by Sir Joshua Reynolds and Thomas Gainsborough.

Frank Sinatra

Sinatra, Frank *b. 1915*

American singer, film star and one of the biggest names in
show business ever since the 1930s when he first became the
'heart throb' of millions of teenagers. It was as a singer with
the Tommy Dorsey band that he made his first film appearance
in *Las Vegas Nights* (1941), and while he suffered a number of
setbacks, continued to grow in stature both on the screen and
on records right through to the 1970s. Some of his greatest
song hits were achieved with the skilled backing of band leader
and arranger Nelson Riddle. Many of his films gave him the
opportunity to develop his talents as dancer and light comedy
actor as well as singer – *Anchors Aweigh* (1945), *On The Town*
(1949), *Guys and Dolls* (1955), *High Society* (1956), *Robin and the
Seven Hoods* (1964). *From Here to Eternity* (1953) and other films
gave him good straight acting parts, and he added another

chapter to his remarkable career with the film series in which he appeared as the hard-bitten, sardonic private detective Tony Rome.

Stanislavsky, Konstantin *1863–1938*

Russian actor and theatre producer who in 1898 was joint founder of the Moscow Arts Theatre. There he put into practice his ideas about method-acting – of thinking deeply about the meaning and truth of the lines to be spoken and dispensing with all unnecessary gestures and other stage effects. He applied his ideas with great success to early productions of Chekhov's plays – *The Seagull, Uncle Vanya, Three Sisters, The Cherry Orchard* – in which he acted as well as produced, and his influence, and that of the Moscow Arts Theatre, soon spread all over the world. Stanislavsky continued his work in the Soviet Union after the Revolution of 1917, and the Moscow Arts Theatre is still a famous institution.

Stewart, James *b. 1908*

American film star, and one of the most popular of all screen personalities. He had been making films for some years before he first rose to real prominence in *The Philadelphia Story* (1940), and from then on was a top box office name. He has been one of the small and distinguished group of actors and actresses to work closely with Alfred Hitchcock (q.v.), starring in *Rope* (1948), *Rear Window* (1954), *The Man Who Knew Too Much* (1955) and *Vertigo* (1958). He also made a big name for himself in such Westerns as *Winchester 73* (1950) and *The Naked Spur* (1953); and he scored another hit in the title role of *The Glenn Miller Story* (1954).

Stroheim, Erich von *1885–1957*

Austrian-born film director and actor. He emigrated to America in 1906 and after playing small parts in such silent film

James Stewart

classics as *The Birth of a Nation* (1915) and *Intolerance* (1916) started to script and direct his own films. He soon emerged in Hollywood as a very talented and original film-maker, but his strong-willed attitude and costly working methods brought him into frequent conflict with others. Nearly all his films were severely cut to bring them down to commercially acceptable lengths, but such productions as *Foolish Wives* (1921) and *Greed* (1923) still give a good account of his brilliance. Later he concentrated more on acting, often playing the part of stiff and aristocratic Prussian officers. In *Sunset Boulevard* (1950) he was Gloria Swanson's (q.v.) equally stiff and unsmiling manservant.

Swanson, Gloria *b. 1898*

American film actress. She first appeared on the screen in 1916 in Mack Sennett (q.v.) comedies, then signed a contract with Cecil B. DeMille (q.v.) who built her up as one of Hollywood's most glamorous stars. During the 1920s she was a celebrated figure, but though she made some successful talkies her personality began to fade. However, in 1950 she made a big comeback, as an ageing Hollywood beauty living on her memories, in *Sunset Boulevard*.

Tarzan

Famous jungle hero, created by Edgar Rice Burroughs whose first Tarzan story was published in 1912. The books were soon followed by a silent feature film – *Tarzan of the Apes* (1918) – and later by an American radio series. Tarzan reached his widest audience with the series of films beginning in 1932 with *Tarzan the Ape Man*, when his celebrated jungle cry first echoed round the world. Johnny Weismuller, an Olympic swimming champion, was the best known screen Tarzan, playing opposite a number of actresses as his tree-top mate, Jane.

Tate, Harry *1872–1940*

British comedian whose real name was Ronald Hutchison – he took his stage name from Henry Tate and Sons, the sugar refining company where he once worked. He specialised in comic sketches about sport, motoring and other pastimes, taking his acts successfully from music hall to revue and pantomime.

Taylor, Elizabeth *b. 1932*

British-born film actress who was evacuated to America during the Second World War and has made her film career largely in Hollywood. During the war she was a child star in such films as *Lassie Come Home* (1943) and *National Velvet* (1944). In the

Richard Burton (q.v.) and Elizabeth Taylor as they appeared in Cleopatra

1950s she emerged as one of the most glamorous young screen actresses of her generation, which led to her being cast in the title role in Cleopatra in 1963 and to the start of her big romance and marriage to Richard Burton (q.v.). They continued their screen partnership through such outstanding films as *The Taming of the Shrew* and the screen version of *Who's Afraid of Virginia Woolf?* (1966) until their marriage broke down in the early 1970s.

Temple, Shirley *b. 1928*

American child film star who first appeared on the screen at the age of four and was soon a phenomenal success with such pictures as *Bright Eyes* (1934), in which she sang and danced 'On the Good Ship Lollipop'. For some years her cuddly charms won hearts all over the world – on her eighth birthday she was reported to have received 135,000 presents – but as she grew up so the magic began to go. She played some teenager roles with fair success but finally left films altogether, to become Mrs Shirley Temple Black – a politician and then an ambassador for her country.

Terry, Dame Ellen *1847–1928*

British actress, and most distinguished member of a famous theatrical family. Early in her career she toured with her sister Kate (grandmother of Sir John Gielgud (q.v.)), married twice, then in 1878 began a long and brilliant stage partnership with Sir Henry Irving (q.v.), performing with him at the London Lyceum theatre and going with him on his American tours. Later in life she gave a series of very fine lectures about Shakespeare, which again took her to America, and her valuable correspondence with Bernard Shaw was published soon after her death. She was made a Dame in 1925.

Tilley, Vesta *1864–1952*

British star of music hall, whose real name was Matilda Powles. She had made her stage debut before the age of four, billed as 'The Great Little Tilley', and over the years developed her act in the great tradition of male impersonators. At the height of her fame she was playing three or four London music halls each night, singing such songs as 'Following in Father's Footsteps', immaculately dressed in top hat and tails. Known as 'The London Idol', Vesta Tilley was also a celebrated principal boy in pantomime.

Tracy, Spencer *1900–1967*

American actor who gave up his medical studies for the stage and made his screen debut in 1930. He used his age to great advantage in the roles he took, progressing from the tough gangster parts of his younger years to portrayals of white-haired statesmen or judges in many of his later films. At the centre of his career was his very popular partnership with

Katharine Hepburn (q.v.), as featured in such box office hits as *Woman of the Year* (1942) and *Adam's Rib* (1949). In his very last film, *Guess Who's Coming to Dinner* (1967), they were together again.

Tree, Sir Herbert Beerbohm *1853–1917*

British actor-manager. He was manager of several famous London theatres, including the Comedy and Haymarket, and built Her Majesty's Theatre, which was completed in 1897. It was there that he staged many of the lavish productions associated both with himself and with the Edwardian age in which he lived. He also founded, in 1904, the Royal Academy of Dramatic Art.

Tucker, Sophie *1884–1966*

American singer, known as 'The Last of the Red Hot Mommas', who accompanied herself at the piano in such songs as 'Some of These Days' and 'Life Begins at Forty'. Her sophisticated, worldly-wise style was as popular in Britain as America.

Tussaud, Marie *1761–1850*

Born Marie Grosholtz and brought up in Switzerland, Madame Tussaud's career was as colourful as that of any of her exhibits. In Paris she learnt the art of wax modelling from her uncle, was employed for some years as an art tutor to the court of Louis XVI at Versailles, and during the bloody aftermath of the Revolution of 1789 had the grim task of making death masks from the heads of some of the distinguished victims of the guillotine. When her marriage failed she came to England with her collection of wax models, touring the British Isles before setting up a permanent exhibition in London. The present museum dates from 1884. Some of Madame Tussaud's original models – of Voltaire, Nelson and other famous people of her own age – have been preserved.

Madame Tussaud

Ustinov, Peter *b. 1921*

British actor, stage and film director and playwright. One of the most versatile artists in show business, Peter Ustinov made his first stage appearance in 1939 doing comic character impersonations – a unique talent which he has developed over the years. He was in the army during the Second World War, but already launched upon his screen career by 1944 when he had a part in the famous British war film *The Way Ahead*. Notable screen performances since then have included Nero in *Quo Vadis?* (1951) and 'Prinny' in *Beau Brummel* (1954). His own plays include *The Love of Four Colonels* (1951). *Romanoff and Juliet* (1956, later made into an attractive film with himself in the central part) and *Photo Finish* (1962). Another film he directed and starred in was an adaptation of Herman Melville's novel about the navy of Nelson's day, *Billy Budd* (1965).

Rudolph Valentino as he appeared in The Sheik

Valentino, Rudolph *1895–1926*

Italian film actor whose full name was Rodolfo Guglielmi di Valentino. He emigrated to America and after a few years as a dancer in night clubs and road shows finally arrived in Hollywood and to sudden stardom in *The Four Horsemen of the Apocalypse* (1921). In this and more especially in *The Sheikh* (1921) he became the screen's great Latin lover. His sudden death was a shock to millions of women all over the world. There were scenes of hysteria at his funeral and a spate of suicides.

Victoria, Vesta *1874–1951*

British star of the Victorian and Edwardian music hall whose songs are among the best-loved of the period – 'Daddy Wouldn't Buy Me a Bow-wow' and 'Waiting at the Church'.

Wallace, Nellie *1870–1948*

British comedienne who began her career as a child clog dancer and then toured the halls with her sisters, billed as the Three Sisters Wallace. On her own she became one of the first and greatest female pantomime Dames. Of her many songs, 'Three Cheers for the Red, White and Blue' is best remembered today.

Waller, Thomas 'Fats' *1904–1943*

Black American pianist, singer and composer. His father was a Baptist minister in Harlem, New York, and young Thomas played the organ in church. He then studied the piano with the great virtuoso pianist Leopold Godowsky before blossoming

Thomas 'Fats' Waller

forth as the exuberant 'Fats' with rolling eyes and jaunty bowler hat, singing such great numbers as 'Ain't Misbehavin', 'Honeysuckle Rose' and 'My Very Good Friend the Milkman'.

Waters, Ethel *b. 1900*

Black American actress and singer. From singing in night clubs and vaudeville she progressed to the Broadway stage in such musical shows as Irving Berlin's *As Thousands Cheer*. She also acted with distinction in *Cabin in the Sky*, *The Member of the Wedding* and other plays. Among the songs she has made famous is the beautiful and moving 'Stormy Weather'.

Wayne, John *1907–1979*

American film actor whose real name was Marion Michael Morrison. He was a football star before going to Hollywood. During the 1930s he played a series of minor film roles until 1939 when he was given a big part in the celebrated Western *Stagecoach*. From then on he was the tough but decent hero of a long line of Hollywood Westerns, including *She Wore a Yellow Ribbon* (1949), *The Man Who Shot Liberty Vallance* (1962) and *True Grit* (1969).

Welles, Orson *b. 1915*

American actor and film director. He was a talented stage actor and director during the 1930s, and in 1938 made a tremendous impact with a vivid radio adaptation of H. G. Wells' story *The*

War of the Worlds. This secured him a Hollywood contract, and he soon made film history with his brilliant direction of *Citizen Kane* (1941) in which he also starred. Subsequent films which he has directed or starred in include *The Magnificent Ambersons* (1942), *The Lady from Shanghai* (1948), *The Third Man* (1949, in which he played the part of Harry Lime), and *The Trail* (1963, based on the novel by Franz Kafka).

West, Mae *b. 1892*

American actress who delighted audiences with the way she made fun of her own sex appeal. Among her many memorable phrases are 'I used to be Snow White but I drifted' and the famous invitation 'Come up and see me some time'. She was a great hit in vaudeville and on the Broadway stage before winning for herself a vast new public on both sides of the Atlantic in such films as *She Done Him Wrong* (1933) and *Belle of the Nineties* (1934). The inflatable life jacket issued to airmen during the Second World War was named after her.

White, Pearl *1889–1938*

American actress and famous star of 'cliff-hanger' serials of the silent film era. She ran away from home after her father had tried to stop her going on the stage, and started appearing in films in 1909. In 1914 she starred as the heroine in *The Perils of Pauline*, a long-running serial that always left her in a desperate situation at the end of each episode. The great success of this production led to several sequels in which Pearl was constantly being snatched from the jaws of death as one episode followed another.

Williams, Bransby *1870–1961*

British character actor whose full name was Bransby William Pharez. He planned to be a missionary and then went into commerce before finally deciding on a stage career. In 1898 he was first seen in a music hall act doing impersonations of famous actors, and soon broadened his repertoire to include impersonations of characters from plays and novels. His Bill Sykes from Dicken's *Oliver Twist* was especially popular. He was equally famous for his recitation of such monologues as 'The Green Eye of the Little Yellow God'. Bransby Williams enjoyed new success on television before dying at the ripe old age of ninety-one.

Wolfit, Sir Donald *1902–1968*

British actor-manager whose name was originally Woolfitt. A man of huge energy and drive, he toured Britain, Canada and other English-speaking countries for many years, performing mainly in Shakespeare. By the Second World War he had formed his own company, and during the Battle of Britain and the Blitz gave hundreds of lunch-time performances in factories and bombed-out towns and cities. Though first and foremost a stage actor, he did make several notable screen appearances, in *Room at the Top* (1958), *Lawrence of Arabia* (1962) and other films. He was knighted in 1957.

Ziegfeld, Florenz *1867–1932*

American showman who was famous for his lavish and spectacular stage shows. He first attracted attention with a show at the Chicago World Fair of 1893. Then he went to London and produced another stage spectacular with Anna Held, the most popular show girl of her day. Back in America he presented the celebrated Ziegfeld Follies that ran for twenty-four years and were the inspiration of several films.

More Beaver Books

We hope you have enjoyed this Beaver Book. Here are some of the other titles:

Famous Lives: Fighting Men A Beaver original. From the siege warfare of Ancient Greece to nuclear holocaust, from Achilles to Zhukov, these are the stories of 176 of the world's most famous warriors. Easy to use and packed with fascinating information, here's a book that's fun to read and useful when you're doing homework! Devised by James Moore, written by Alan Blackwood and illustrated by Peter Dennis.

Famous Lives: Scientists and Inventors A Beaver original. Want to know who invented the saxophone, or who discovered the electron? Read all about the amazing achievements of 180 great scientists and inventors from ancient times right down to today. Devised by James Moore, written by Norman Dahl and illustrated by Peter Dennis.

The Beaver Book of Pets A Beaver original. A love of animals just isn't enough to help you look after pets properly. This book tells you how to choose the right pet, how to feed, house and handle it, what it will cost to keep, even how to tell when it's ill. There are detailed chapters on dogs, cats, rabbits, guinea pigs, mice, hamsters, gerbils, birds, horses and ponies, reptiles, fish, insects and wild animals. Written by Raymond Chaplin and illustrated with both black and white photographs and drawings by Tony Morris.

337111